BEHIND THE NEWS

SCHOOL SHOOTINGS

Philip Steele

WAYLAND

The publisher would would like to thank the
following for their kind permission to reproduce
their photographs:

Shutterstock.com unless stated otherwise:
Front cover: © Lastdays1, Sascha Burkard, Ron Frank
© Dmcdesign (5), © Irina Alyakina (7), PETER
CLOSE (8 – posed by model), Patrick McCall (9),
WIKI_Commons (10), REX/ZUMA (11), MANDY
GODBEHEAR (13- posed by model), © Tommaso79
(13- posed by model), Vartanov Anatoly (14),
kilukilu (15), © Reuters/CORBIS (16), © Michael
Corrigan (18), Paul Drabot (19), bikeriderlondon
(20), Ryan Rodrick Beiler (21), REX (22), REX/Drew
Farrell (23), Gregory Johnston (24) © Richard
Gunion (25), Kodda (26), © EDUARDO MUNOZ/
Reuters/Corbis (27), WIKI_Commons © Cubico (29),
360b (29), Sascha Burkard (31), Gina Jacobs (31),
wellphoto (32), © MICHELLE MCLOUGHLIN/
Reuters/Corbis (33), Youtube_Wellington Menezes
de Oliveira (34), REX/KeystoneUSA-ZUMA (35),
WIKI_Escola Tasso da Silveira Licença Creative
Commons Atribuição 3.0 Brasil (35), © Gordon M.
Grant/Splash News/Corbis (37), 3 trekandshoot
(38), © AARON JOSEFCZYK/Reuters/Corbis (39), ©
Mugglewizard (41), Gina Jacobs (42), Wiki_Virginia
Tech Balloons released over NEZ GNU Free
Documentation License (43), © Rmarmion (44),
© Sean Pavone (45).

CONTENTS

DEATH IN THE CLASSROOM

The images from the security cameras look grim. Children are running for their lives or hiding behind desks. A shadowy figure raises a gun. The television news shows the world outside – police, sobbing parents, reporters. 'Another school shooting...'

The shock of terror

Any attack on a school is a terrible event to see on the news, and an even more terrible event to witness in your local community. The shock is heightened because the victims are young children, teenagers or students – innocent people with their lives ahead of them. A school or college is supposed to be a place of education, a refuge for civilised values.

We are not talking about fist fights here, but about knives, deadly handguns,

The Global Profile

CONTINENT	INCIDENTS	NUMBERS KILLED
North America		
Canada	9	26
USA	297	137
Mexico	2	2
South America	2	17
Europe	17	63
Asia	9	66
Africa	2	51
Oceania	6	5

Figures from 1980–2012

rifles – even home-made bombs. The attacks may take place in a classroom or hall, a playground or school bus, or a college campus. They threaten the lives of pupils, teachers, staff, passers-by, police and paramedics.

So many questions

Our immediate question is why? So many other questions arise. Who could do such a thing? How could it happen? How can such attacks be prevented? And above all, how can any survivors, friends or parents cope with such trauma or loss?

Then, we worry about the bigger picture. How common are school attacks? What is the scale of the problem? Are they more common in some parts of the world than others? Do they generally occur in a particular type of neighbourhood or community? Have they always taken place, or is this something new? In this book, we go behind the news to try and find some answers to these questions.

People gather in Burlington, Vermont, USA, for a candlelit vigil held in memory of the victims of a school shooting in nearby Newtown in 2012.

Leabharlanna Poiblí Chathair Baile Átha Cliath

THE LONGER VIEW

Many people believe that the problem of school killings is rooted in the nature of society today. That may well be true, but the issue is not a new one. The following stories from history sound chillingly similar to modern tragedies.

Past events

• *Back in 1853, a student in Louisville, Kentucky, USA, shot dead a teacher who had punished his brother.*

• *In 1909, after an incident in Nevada City, California, USA, a newspaper article pointed out that even young boys were carrying handguns into school.*

• *The USA's worst ever school killing took place in 1927. A former school official blew up Bath Elementary School, Michigan. He killed 38 pupils and six adults on and off the site, and injured 58 more.*

People stare in shock at the ruins of Bath Elementary School, Michigan, after the explosion which killed 44 people in 1927.

Personal reasons

History shows that, just as today, there were many different reasons for school killings. Many were personal, perhaps from quarrels or personal relationships.

- *In 1884, a teacher in Markdale, Ontario, Canada, shot his assistant when she turned down his marriage proposal, and then killed himself.*

Mental issues

Many school killings were carried out by adults who suffered from severe mental illness or breakdown. This was particularly tragic if a teacher, the person caring for the children's welfare, turned killer.

- *In 1902, a schoolmaster in Bohemia, Austria-Hungary, seized a revolver from his desk and started shooting at random, killing three pupils and seriously wounding three others, before being killed by some villagers who had rushed to the scene.*

Violent regions

History also shows that many of the most terrible killings in schools occur in a region that is experiencing a wider conflict. These conflicts can range from a war to a sustained terrorist campaign, a prolonged hostage crisis or violent gang warfare on the streets. Such violent situations are still common today.

- *In 2004, Chechen separatists in Russia held 1,100 people hostage in a school at Beslan, including 777 pupils. As the siege was ended by security forces, 186 children lost their lives.*

Flowers are left at the ruins of Beslan school, Russia, on the anniversary of tragedy when Chechen separatists took hundreds of school children hostage.

PROFILING KILLERS

There are many more deaths related to firearms in the USA than in other developed countries. One reason for this is the large number of high-profile mass shootings. The number of school shootings, in particular, has risen sharply in recent decades.

Searching for reasons

Killers are often portrayed as 'evil monsters', or as 'loners', 'misfits' or 'losers'. In reality, the things that turn people to these extreme acts of violence are multiple and complex, both psychological and social. Many perpetrators suffer feelings of low self-esteem and fear of failure. Home life may be under increasing pressure with money worries or a lost job.

Children may come from homes where there is abuse or violence. Some may feel excluded from friendship groups because of their appearance, race, class or poverty.

People who have trouble fitting in and spend lots of time on their own may have feelings of isolation, which could lead to them becoming violent.

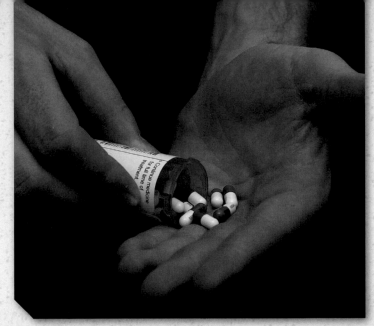

The use of drugs, both legal and illegal, could push people into crime and lead to them developing violent tendencies.

Many have a history of isolation, of being treated as outsiders, of being bullied. Bullying and cruelty are no longer limited to the classroom and playground, having found new outlets on social media or through mobile phones.

Mental health

Psychological problems may be aggravated by real or imagined grievances. Some people believe that medications, which are increasingly prescribed to deal with mental health problems, such as antipsychotic drugs or antidepressants, may be partly to blame. These can sometimes make people feel suicidal and violent. Many mass killers end their rampage by committing suicide.

The Global Profile

KILLERS...
• Nearly all those who carry out school killings are male.
• More than a third are aged over 11 and under 18. More than 20 per cent fall into the college student age group (19 to 25). That leaves a large number of adult killers.

... AND VICTIMS
• Secondary or high schools are the most common targets, followed by universities and colleges, with primary or elementary schools after that.
• Females are more likely to be killed than males.
• Over a quarter of victims are teachers or other school staff.

SANDY HOOK, 2012

On the morning of 14 December 2012, Adam Lanza of Newtown, Connecticut, USA, shot his mother Nancy dead and then drove to an elementary school he had once attended. The school, in the community of Sandy Hook, was securely locked to outsiders.

NEWS FLASH

Date: 14 December 2012
Location: Newtown, Connecticut, USA
Target: Sandy Hook Elementary School
Perpetrator: Adam Lanza (aged 20)
Deaths: 28 including the perpetrator and his mother
Injured: 2
Outcome: Suicide

The whole attack, from the time Lanza entered the school until his suicide, took just 10 minutes.

The attack

At 9.35 am, Lanza shot his way through a glass door. He shot dead the head teacher and a child psychologist. Lanza then burst into a first-grade classroom, killing a supply teacher, a teaching assistant and 15 children. One six-year-old girl survived by pretending to be dead. In another classroom, Lanza shot five more children, their teacher and another assistant. Other teachers hid pupils in cupboards and under desks, and barricaded doors.

Local and state police responded rapidly. Police began to work their way

Teachers lead crying children away from Sandy Hook Elementary School in the aftermath of the attack.

through the building, clearing rooms and leading terrified children to safety. Nearby Danbury Hospital was put on emergency alert. As soon as the police moved in, Lanza shot himself in the head.

The aftermath

The grief of parents and friends of the victims was raw. Flowers and tributes were left and vigils were held in churches. US President Barack Obama attended a vigil in memory of the victims and vowed to regulate firearms, starting off a fierce political debate. Shockwaves spread from Sandy Hook across the USA and around the world.

'Our daughter Grace was the love and light of our family.'

Message among the candles at the Sandy Hook vigil for Grace McDonnell, 7.

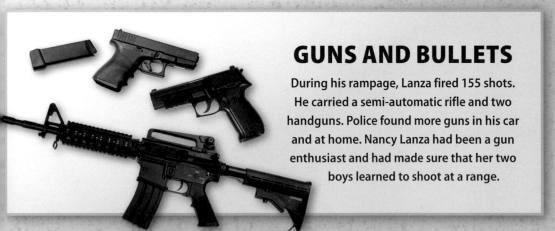

GUNS AND BULLETS

During his rampage, Lanza fired 155 shots. He carried a semi-automatic rifle and two handguns. Police found more guns in his car and at home. Nancy Lanza had been a gun enthusiast and had made sure that her two boys learned to shoot at a range.

WHAT ARE THE MORAL ISSUES?

Moral principles are those that categorise behaviour as right or wrong. Mass murder is regarded as immoral and as a crime. This view is reflected in law, but courts also recognise that mental illness may reduce a killer's ability to make a moral judgment.

'We are in a state of disbelief and trying to find whatever answers we can. We, too, are asking why?'

Peter Lanza, estranged father of Sandy Hook killer Adam Lanza, as reported in *The New York Times*.

Murder and morals

Religious scriptures also condemn murder, although some faiths may legitimise other forms of killing innocent people, as in warfare. Are some types of killing worse than others? After the Sandy Hook massacre, a small group of Christians claimed that the killer was doing God's will, in punishing America for its immoral ways. This contorted reasoning shocked other Christians and the wider community, being deeply offensive to relatives of the victims.

Pressures at school

Schools are often emotional pressure cookers for young people, for many reasons. Schools impose rules, they make demands, and they are full of adolescent insecurity and peer group pressure. Most people learn to cope with this during their school career, but, in a few cases, school days may leave emotional scars which last a lifetime. That may be why schools become targets for violent attacks – they appear to be a symbol of all that is wrong in one's life.

Bullying and alienation at school can come at a time when children are feeling very insecure about themselves. This can increase their feelings of isolation.

'We don't have a crime problem, a gun problem or even a violence problem. What we have is a sin problem.'

Mike Huckabee, former Governor of Arkansas and host of a show on *FOX News, USA.*

The moral issues around school killings are very simple – they are terrible crimes. However, the complexity of the human mind and social interaction mean that many questions must be debated in order for the problem to be dealt with properly.

A CARING SOCIETY?

To what extent should wider society share responsibility for school killings? If medications, which can sometimes lead to episodes of extreme violence, are being over-prescribed for depression or behavioural problems, are the doctors or the pharmaceutical companies also at fault? If the perpetrator has been bullied at school, are other children or school authorities responsible to some degree for the crime?

A VIOLENT WORLD

Are school killings part of a major social breakdown? People worry about security and build gated communities, which only encourages isolation. They hear exaggerated reports of crime – and, in some places, they buy guns to protect themselves.

Cultures of violence

Throughout the 20th century, films and television glorified gun battles in the Wild West, and made stars out of mobsters and mafia killers. The killings were often divorced from any sense of reality or consequence, as played out by children in playgrounds, yelling with pointed fingers:

SCHOOL VIOLENCE IN THE USA

A 2011 survey of pupils from grades 9 to 12 revealed the following:

- 12 per cent had been in a physical fight in the previous 12 months.
- 5.9 per cent had not gone into school on one or more days in the previous month, fearing for their safety.
- 5.4 per cent had carried a knife, club or gun in school premises at some time in the previous month.
- 7.4 per cent reported being threatened or injured with a weapon on school premises at some time during the previous month.

'Bang-bang – you're dead'. Today, the obsession with violence has become global. Children and adults spend hours playing computer games based on shooting guns and hunting down victims.

Television and online news channels also bring real-life images of warfare, terrorism and other violent events into the sitting room, making carnage seem almost normal.

Copycat terror

Images of shooting and violence are everywhere, but, of course, not all the viewers turn into killers. However, the effect on just a few troubled people might well be very deep. Feeling inadequate, they seek celebrity. Feeling hard done by, they look for revenge. We do know that some have been inspired by footage of other school shootings.

ERIC HARRIS   DYLAN KLEBOLD

SUSPECTS   CNN

A TV news channel flashes up images of Eric Harris and Dylan Klebold, who were responsible for the Columbine High School shootings in 1999 (see pages 16–17). Theories about what motivated them include bullying, psychological problems and the influence of violent computer games.

'Rather than a loss of innocence, I've got to hope that something like this encourages us to be better people.'

US President Bill Clinton at the dedication of the Columbine Memorial Park.

COLUMBINE, 1999

The massacre of pupils and one teacher at Columbine, Colorado, left yet another community devastated. More than any other, Columbine came to symbolise the horror of school killings. The killers shouted, laughed and taunted their victims as they gunned them down.

NEWS FLASH

Date: 20 April 1999
Location: Columbine, Colorado, USA
Target: Columbine High School
Perpetrators: Eric Harris (left, aged 18), Dylan Klebold (right, aged 17)
Deaths: 15 including both perpetrators
Injured: 21
Outcome: Double suicide

The killers planned to use 99 explosive devices, including pipe bombs and firebombs, as well as guns.

Ruthless murderers

Eric Harris and Dylan Klebold began their deadly attack by placing a small firebomb in a field near their high school, in order to divert the emergency services. They then drove to the school and placed two propane bombs hidden in bags in the cafeteria. When the bombs failed to explode, the two returned and, at 11.19 am, began shooting and scattering pipe bombs. The police were called at 11.22 am and engaged in a gun battle with Harris. The two killers entered the library where pupils were hiding and

CCTV footage captures Eric Harris and Dylan Klebold during their rampage through Columbine High School.

'I have a goal to destroy as much as possible, so I must not be sidetracked by my feelings of sympathy, mercy or any of that.'

Eric Harris, journal entry.

opened fire. The attackers later returned to the school cafeteria and tried to detonate the bombs. They committed suicide at about 12.08 pm.

Getting to the truth

Television crews rushed to the scene. News of the tragedy spread around the world. Many of the reports included more hearsay and speculation than actual facts. It was said that the two had been bullied, that they were loners, that they had been prescribed antidepressants, that they were in a gang, that they were influenced by violent computer games or by controversial 'satanic' rock performers, such as Marilyn Manson. A decade after the massacre, it became clear that many of those stories were untrue or exaggerated.

The two killers were deeply disturbed individuals. One official report suggests Harris was a psychopath, while Klebold was extremely depressed. Their aim was to create a major terrorist attack.

'I wouldn't say a single word to them. I would listen to what they have to say and that's what no one did.'

Marilyn Manson, when asked what he would say to the Columbine killers.

DO GAMES MAKE US VIOLENT?

The experience of real-life violence and fear can obviously affect human behaviour during childhood and later. But what about made-up violence on film, television or computer games? Does it really play a part in school killings such as Columbine?

Many video games use replica guns as part of their playing experience.

'... continued exposure to violent videos will make an adolescent less sensitive to violence, more accepting of violence, and more likely to commit aggressive acts.'

Dr Jordan Grafman, US National Institutes of Health study.

Violence and fantasy

Some experts believe that made-up violence does play a part, and that immersion in realistic and violent games can be dangerous for some people. Others disagree and claim that indulging in fantasy violence may actually reduce incidence of the real thing. Parents are often advised to monitor their children's game activities and to look out for any signs of trouble.

From screen to missile

Some point out that the line between computer games and actual warfare is beginning to be blurred. Missiles or drones can be deployed by an operator sitting at a desk. Warfare has become impersonal, a mere screen image.

The campaigning film director Michael Moore made a successful movie called *Bowling for Columbine* (2002), which looked into some of the possible causes behind the attack. In the movie, he pointed out that the industrial giant Lockheed Martin, which makes missiles and unmanned attack systems, has a base at Littleton, near Columbine. Could connections be made with the school shooting? Not a direct one, maybe, but the comparison does raise important moral questions. Are national institutions, economies and global politics also based on violence and fear? Does school killing fit into a global jigsaw puzzle of violence?

Drone operators can destroy targets on the other side of the world, without any risk to their own lives.

DEBATE

Does exposure to violence in computer games lead to real-life violence?

YES
They make a person less sensitive to violence.

NO
We need to look at real-life causes.

CONTROLLING GUN NUMBERS

Mental health problems, social problems, and a culture of violence: these are issues that are common in many countries. So why do most school shootings occur in the USA? The extra factors that tip the balance are the easy availability and social acceptance of guns.

> **'A well regulated militia, being necessary to the security of a free state, the right of the people to keep and bear arms, shall not be infringed.'**
>
> **Second Amendment to the US Constitution.**

The gun business

The USA has the highest ownership of guns in the world. Nearly half the population keep one or more guns on their property. Although the US population only makes up five per cent of the world's total, between 35 and 50 per cent of all the world's civilian-owned guns are found in that country.

In the USA, guns and ammunition can be bought over the counter in shops like this one, in supermarkets or online.

Pro-gun organisations in the US, such as the Second Amendment Sisters, campaign to preserve the right to carry guns.

Carrying guns

US law permits far wider gun ownership than in other countries. In fact, ever since 1791, the right of US citizens to keep and carry arms has been guaranteed under the Second Amendment to the US Constitution. At the time, this provision was intended to empower citizens' militias (military forces raised from the civilian population). In 2008, the US Supreme Court interpreted the words to mean that any US citizen had the right to own a weapon. Many Americans hold strongly to this right, which is supported by the arms industry and by the five-million-strong National Rifle Association.

Gun control

Many other Americans argue powerfully for gun control, especially in the wake of mass shootings. They face an uphill political struggle. After the Sandy Hook massacre, President Barack Obama proposed tighter background checks, smaller ammunition magazines and the prohibition of some types of rifle. In April 2013, the US Senate voted down these proposals.

The Global Profile

GUN OWNERSHIP AROUND THE WORLD
AVERAGE FIREARMS PER 100 POPULATION (2007)

- Argentina 10.2 • Australia 15 • Canada 30.8 • China 4.9
- England and Wales 6.2 • Scotland 5.5 • Finland 45.3 • France 31.2
- Germany 30.3 • India 4.2 • Japan 0.6 • Russia 8.9
- Switzerland 45.7 • United States 89.0

DUNBLANE, 1996

Thomas Hamilton had been a scout leader, but had been removed from this post on the suspicion of inappropriate behaviour towards young boys. He complained that the rumours were false and he became bitterly aggrieved, even writing to the Queen.

NEWS FLASH

Date: 13 March 1996
Location: Dunblane, Scotland, UK
Target: Dunblane Primary School
Perpetrator: Thomas Hamilton (aged 43)
Deaths: 18 including the perpetrator
Injured: 15
Outcome: Suicide

During the attack at the Dunblane Primary School, Thomas Hamilton fired a total of 109 shots.

The tragedy

On 13 March 1996, Hamilton entered the primary school in Dunblane, to the north of Stirling in Scotland. He went to the gym and shot dead 15 five- and six-year-old children. Their teacher, Gwen Mayor, was

'This is a slaughter of the innocents, unlike anything we have seen in Scotland...'

Scottish Member of Parliament Helen Liddell, 1996.

Parents and children wait anxiously outside the gates of Dunblane Primary School to find out news of what has happened inside.

killed trying to protect them. Hamilton then raked a mobile classroom with bullets, but the children had already hidden under tables. He fired into a corridor and then returned to the gym, where he shot himself. He was armed with weapons he owned legally – two pistols and two revolvers.

Parents gathered outside the school to await the grim news. Among them was Judy Murray, mother of the future tennis stars Jamie and Andy Murray, who were then ten and eight years old respectively and pupils at the school.

UK gun control

Some parents set up the Snowdrop Petition to ban private ownership of guns, and this was signed by 705,000 people. A press campaign gathered a further 428,279 signatures. A public inquiry was held and, as a result, the government introduced a ban on all cartridge-ammunition handguns, of the type used by Hamilton, apart from .22 calibre single-shot guns. However, these were also banned in 1997.

'These terrible events present a sort of once-in-a-lifetime opportunity to turn the gun laws round.'

Gill Marshall-Andrews of Gun Control Network talks to Paul Waldie of the Canadian *Globe and Mail*, 2012.

WHAT IS THE BEST POLICY?

In the USA, the pro-gun lobby regards the Second Amendment (see pages 20–21) as a civil right, at the heart of the American way of life.

'The only thing that stops a bad guy with a gun is a good guy with a gun.'

Wayne LaPierre, National Rifle Association.

Pro-gun protestors campaign to keep the Second Amendment, telling politicians to 'stick to their guns' and claiming it is their right to carry weapons.

'Guns are not the problem, people are...'

Pro-gun campaigners claim that if everyone could use guns, then crime rates would fall. They believe that gun control can never fully work and that it would make more sense if people were taught how to use weapons responsibly. Some point out that current policing is too poorly funded to be effective on its own. When it comes to mass shootings and school killings, they say the problem is not availability of guns but issues of mental health screening.

'How many have to die before we will give up these dangerous toys?'

Stephen King, Guns (2013).

Supporters of gun control stand outside the White House, asking the president to 'put gun control on the agenda' and 'save our children'.

'As long as guns are there, they will be used to kill...'

The counter-arguments run on these lines. The Second Amendment has been misinterpreted: the right to bear arms was not conferred upon individuals but on 'well-regulated militias', a context that is in any case over two centuries out of date. In a democracy, disputes should be settled peacefully and lawfully, not by a gun. If policing is ineffective, then the answer is to ensure that it works properly, not to allow people to act as unaccountable vigilantes. Recent studies show that societies with a high handgun ownership are not safer, but more violent. Mental health issues are important, but if the guns were not there, they could not be used.

America divided

The divide is often a bitter one, with powerful organisations acting on both sides. Members of the National Rifle Association have regularly and effectively campaigned in the face of protests by victims of school killings.

GUN CONTROL POLL

After the 2012 massacre in Newtown, Connecticut, a poll showed that 58 per cent supported tighter gun control. By September 2013, that support had fallen to 49 per cent. Victims' fears that, yet again, no action would be taken seemed to be well founded.

SAFE SCHOOLS

School killings, like earthquakes or volcanic eruptions, are very hard to predict. Who knows the exact moment when a disturbed child or adult will finally lose control and tip over the edge? But every warning sign has to be noted.

Profiling students?

It is not easy and probably not sensible to profile all students in order to highlight potential killers. Many of the children in a school will suffer from bullying and depression or have difficulty making social contacts. Many will fight, and many will watch violent computer games or television programmes. Yet they will never be killers and may well grow up to be happy and confident adults with children of their own. Parents, teachers and other

SURVEILLANCE SOCIETY?

- About 75 per cent of British teachers now work in schools equipped with security cameras. Ely College in Cambridgeshire, UK , has one camera for every ten pupils.
- In the USA, more than 60 per cent of state schools have security cameras.
- There is little evidence to show that cameras reduce violence in schools. Some people believe the violence simply moves to areas not covered by cameras. However, several school killers have been caught on camera.

children in the school just have to be alert and report all unusual threats, boasts, gun obsessions or other extreme behaviour from their classmates or those who are in their care.

Making schools secure

Teachers also have to be well drilled in emergency procedures, knowing how to evacuate a school and protect its pupils. Boundary defences, cameras and metal detectors already make it harder for the public to gain access to schools – and not just in the USA. Teachers need to be checked against criminal records, to ensure that children are safe in their class.

Arms in the school?

After the massacre at Newtown, Connecticut, USA, in 2012 (see pages 10–11), many more US schools began to deploy armed security guards or police on the school premises. In some US states, even the teachers were armed with guns and given weapons training. The gun lobby declared that schools that did not do this were setting themselves up as potential victims and open to an attack, thereby threatening the safety of the children inside. This argument was strongly opposed by many people, including parents, teachers and relatives of the victims.

Following the attacks on Sandy Hook Elementary School in Newtown, Connecticut, many US towns placed armed police at schools in their area.

WINNENDEN, 2009

A pre-agreed coded security message was broadcast around the Albertville secondary school in Winnenden, Germany, on 11 March 2009. 'Frau Koma is coming.' Koma is 'amok' spelt backwards, and it signalled that a killer was on the loose.

NEWS FLASH

Date: 11 March 2009
Location: Winnenden, Germany
Target: Albertville-Realschule
Perpetrator: Tim Kretschmer (aged 17)
Deaths: 17 including the perpetrator
Injured: 7 in Winneden, 2 in Wendlingen
Outcome: Suicide

Kretschmer announced his attack hours beforehand in Internet chatrooms.

'For fun, because it's fun.'

Tim Kretschmer explains his motive to Igor Wolf.

Girls targeted

The shooter was Tim Kretschmer, a former pupil armed with a semi-automatic pistol he had taken from his parents' bedroom.

He was dressed in black combat gear. The warning came too late for a teacher and nine teenagers (eight of them girls) in the first two classrooms.

Kretschmer murdered them all. Within three minutes the police were alerted. They took two minutes to arrive at the school. Kretschmer escaped, killing two more women teachers on the way out. Most of his victims were female, and this seemed to be part of his plan. The gunman then killed a caretaker outside a nearby hospital and hijacked a car, holding the driver, Igor Wolf, at gunpoint as he drove to nearby Wendlingen. Three more died there in gun battles before Kretschmer shot himself.

Depression and anger

Tim Kretschmer had consulted a therapist about his depression, anger and thoughts of violence. Kretschmer's father was also a member of a shooting club, and 15 more guns were found at the family home in Leutenbach.

'Incomprehensible... It is an appalling crime.'

German Chancellor Angela Merkel speaking after the attack.

A NATION MOURNS

German Chancellor Angela Merkel said after the attack that 'this is a day of mourning for the whole of Germany'. A minute's silence was held at the European Parliament and all German flags were flown at half-mast until 13 March in memory of the victims.

DO WE NEED GUNS IN SCHOOLS?

Securing school premises clearly makes good sense, and being prepared for the unthinkable to happen is essential. However, it is important that the right balance is struck.

'The possibility of an armed presence in our schools is a deterrent.'

US Representative Scott Craig, Rapid City.

What is best for the children?

Educational psychologists advise that excessive or intrusive surveillance does not necessarily make for a good environment for learning or care. Reinforcing fear or anxiety may have exactly the opposite effect to the one intended. Children need privacy and trust. It is important, too, that strictly controlled access to school premises does not isolate it from the surrounding community.

Guns in or guns out?

The biggest security question of all is whether to allow guns into schools in order to protect children from attack.

DEBATE
Should we allow guns in school to protect children?

YES
It can end a rampage swiftly and works as a deterrent.

NO
It goes against core principles of education and is dangerous.

Messages placed at a memorial to the victims of the Sandy Hook massacre express the thoughts and wishes of friends and neighbours.

In the USA, this practice was introduced in some states after the massacre at Newtown, Connecticut. It is a move regarded as essential by the pro-gun lobby, who argue that only an on-site armed response can end a rampage swiftly. In 2013, even the Obama government, no friend of the gun lobby, put millions of dollars into a scheme for placing armed police officers in schools.

Most people supporting gun control, in the USA and around the world, call for schools to be gun-free. They do not want guns to be normalised and argue that arming teachers goes against core education principles, and is also dangerous. History has shown that teachers may also suffer from problems, and that involving inexperienced teachers in gun battles places pupils and other teachers at risk.

DRUG FREE

GUN FREE
SCHOOL
ZONE

A sign shows that this school is a drug and weapon free zone.

'The idea that because the problem is guns, the answer is guns, is simply ridiculous. I think it reflects more that some people take every opportunity to expand the gun trade.'

Dick North, whose daughter was killed in the Dunblane massacre, 2012.

MEDIA MATTERS

We live in an age that values social media profiles, celebrity and fame at any cost. To a young man suffering from low self-esteem and a desire to get his own back on society, even mass murder can be a way of getting the recognition he craves.

'... people have the option of picking facts according to their political beliefs, instead of the other way round. The current debate over gun control is a testament to this trend.'

Walker Bragman in *The Huffington Post*, 2013.

TV news crews and presenters and other journalists will descend on the scene of a shooting to report events and get them on screen, online or in print as quickly as possible.

In the wake of the intrusive behaviour of journalists following the school shooting in Newtown, Connecticut, local people posted this message comparing reporters to vultures – birds that feed on the dead.

A part of the problem?

Is the media fanning the flames of school killings by turning the perpetrators into household names? In 2013, an English teenager was accused of planning to attack his former school with guns and pipe bombs. It was said he wanted to recreate the horrors of the Columbine massacre. School killers do tend to be inspired by earlier tragedies and plan copycat killings.

Mixed media

The coverage of school shootings is a reflection of political and cultural opinion and can vary from one newspaper or television channel to another. Some debates are sensationalist, others more considered and thoughtful. Some journalism is investigative. In most European countries, the call for strict gun control is more widespread, whereas in the USA, gun enthusiasts are more vocal in the press, on television and online. They were strong critics of the best-known American film on school killings, Michael Moore's *Bowling for Columbine* (2002), which called for much tighter gun control. In it, Moore takes victims of the Columbine massacre to the local supermarket, to demand that the store removes ammunition from its shelves.

REALENGO, 2011

Rio de Janeiro is all too familiar with gun crime, but this was Brazil's first school shooting. Plans to implement a gun reduction scheme in the city were stepped up, although the chief target here was gang warfare, not school shootings.

NEWS FLASH

Date: 7 April 2011
Location: Realengo, Rio de Janeiro, Brazil
Target: Tasso da Silveira Municipal School
Perpetrator: Wellington Menezes de Oliveira (aged 23)
Deaths: 13 including the perpetrator
Injured: 12
Outcome: Suicide

Wellington Menezes de Oliveira killed 12 children, ten of whom were girls.

The victims

At 8.30 am on 7 April 2011, Wellington Oliveira, a former pupil of Tasso da Silveira Municipal School, an elementary school in the working-class suburb of Realengo, was allowed into the school to check his school records. Instead, he went up to an eighth grade classroom and took out two revolvers. He then shot 12 pupils dead, aged 12 to 14 years. Two police officers rushed into the school and, before Wellington could reach the next floor, they shot and wounded him. He fell down a flight of stairs before committing

A wounded pupil is carried out of the Tasso da Silveira Municipal School following Oliveira's attack.

suicide. Wounded children were ferried to hospital by helicopter, which landed on a nearby football pitch.

A history of bullying

Wellington was an adopted child who had been a very inward-looking pupil at school, and repeatedly bullied. Raised as a Jehovah's Witness, he later converted to Islam. His head was full of religious notions and rituals. He had lost his job in 2010 and had few friends.

'He was a very lonely person... He was always isolated and in his own world.'

Neighbour Elda Lira, aged 55.

NATIONAL RESPONSE

The events surrounding Oliveira's attack on the school (left) shocked the whole Brazilian nation. This was the first time that a mass shooting had taken place that was not linked to gang activities. The president declared three days of national mourning and announced a disarmament programme that would run until the end of 2011.

HOW SHOULD THE MEDIA ACT?

While the news needs to be reported and the perpetrators need to be named, sensationalist or excessive coverage may only impress and encourage other killers or stoke up public fear. Is it permissible to broadcast images of such a tragic event?

News and ethics

Rolling news reports – and the consequent need to fill in long periods with new developments in a story – mean that speculation and rumour are often presented as fact. This happened at Columbine and again at Newtown, Connecticut. Careless reporting can

A JOURNALIST:

• At all times upholds and defends the principle of media freedom, the right of freedom of expression and the right of the public to be informed.

• Strives to ensure that information is honestly conveyed, accurate and fair.

• Does nothing to intrude into anybody's private life, grief or distress unless justified by overriding consideration of the public interest.

• Shall normally seek the consent of an appropriate adult when interviewing or photographing a child for a story about his or her welfare.

Articles from the Code of Conduct, National Union of Journalists (UK)

sometimes misdirect public anger, or point blame at innocent people, or place undue emphasis on certain aspects of the perpetrator's character.

Respect for the victims

A major difficulty arises with interviewing parents, relatives and neighbours of victims. It is all too easy to intrude at the very moment when they need private space to deal with their shock and grief. Children can only be interviewed with parental permission, and even then need to be treated with the greatest care and thoughtfulness.

A good reporter gets these things right, but the urgency, nature and format of television news opens up many pitfalls.

Online, the informality of social media sites and blogs is open to abuse, as anger and rumour feed conspiracy theories, misinformation, political squabbling – and lack of respect for the victims.

Mourners grieve at a memorial site in Newtown, Connecticut, next to a sign asking journalists and camera crews to keep away.

NO MEDIA BEYOND THIS POINT

INFO CALL:
203-270-4276

PREVENTING ATTACKS

On 19 March 2013, Thomas 'TJ' Lane was sentenced to three life sentences without parole. In 2012, aged 17, he had shot and killed three pupils and injured three others at the Chardon High School in the US state of Ohio.

Crime and punishment

Murder carries extremely grave penalties in jurisdictions around the world, depending on the circumstances. In the case of school killings, relevant factors include the mental state and the age of the accused. The age of criminal responsibility in the UK is 18. In the USA, it varies from state to state. No countries within the European Union allow the death penalty. In the USA, 32 of

While the threat of a prison sentence may act as a deterrent for most crimes, many people argue that is ineffective in preventing school shootings.

At his trial, TJ Lane showed no remorse. He took off his shirt to show the word 'killer' written on his prison T-shirt. He smirked and offered obscene abuse to the relatives of his victims.

the 50 states allow capital punishment, but, since 2005, only those aged 18 and above at the time of the crime can be given the death penalty. Killers who are too young or mentally disturbed may be detained in secure institutions rather than held inside a prison.

Suicidal outcomes

School killings are unusual because so many of them end in suicide. In these cases, justice cannot take its legal course, and punishment may not be a deterrent if the perpetrator's intention is their own death. When this happens, the chief aim of the law has to be to prevent the crime in the first place and so save lives. In other outcomes, the killer may be shot dead by the police during the rampage.

'No single law – no set of laws – can eliminate evil from the world, or prevent every senseless act of violence in our society. But that can't be an excuse for inaction. Surely, we can do better than this.'

US President Barack Obama.

VIRGINIA TECH, 2007

The Virginia Tech massacre of 2007 was the worst attack by a single gunman in American history. It raised many questions about loopholes in the law which allowed the warning signs to be missed.

NEWS FLASH

Date: 16 April 2007
Location: Blacksburg, Virginia, USA
Target: Virginia Polytechnic Institute and State University
Perpetrator: Seung-Hui Cho (aged 23)
Deaths: 33 including the perpetrator
Injured: 23
Outcome: Suicide

During the second attack on the Engineering, Science and Mechanics department, Cho fired more than 170 bullets.

'We must double our efforts to reduce easy access to guns and take more seriously the need to address mental disorders and mental depression.'

Reverend Jesse Jackson, civil rights activist.

Crime scene tape surrounds Norris Hall, Virginia Tech, the scene of Cho's first attack.

Attacks on campus

The killer was a senior student, Seung-Hui Cho, a South Korean citizen who lived permanently in the United States. He launched two separate attacks on the campus, armed with two handguns. The first was in a hall of residence, where he shot two students. He then went to his room, changed his clothes, removed his computer's hard drive and mailed videos and writings he had made to the broadcaster NBC. He then went to the Engineering, Science and Mechanics department, chaining the door shut behind him. In this second terrifying attack, he killed another 30 people, including five members of the academic staff. He then committed suicide.

The warnings ignored

Cho had suffered from anxiety attacks, depression and speech difficulties. He was said to have been bullied, too, but this was not confirmed. When he went to Virginia Tech, psychiatric reports were not forwarded because of privacy laws. His mental problems continued, but because of differences between state and federal procedures, he was not barred from purchasing firearms. The massacre also raised concerns about the legal responsibilities of college administrations, as well as gun laws and the ethics of the different parts of the media.

WHAT HAPPENS AFTERWARDS?

Justice is a bigger issue than the provisions of the law or methods of policing. It goes further than the lawsuits for millions of dollars filed by the victims' families against Virginia Tech for alleged failures in their duties of student care.

'Our collective strength and resilience will serve as an example to the rest of the world.'

Charles Dumais, principal Newtown High School, Connecticut, USA.

A memorial created following the massacre at Sandy Hook Elementary School in Newtown, Connecticut, lists the names of the victims of the attack, describing them as 'heroes'.

NEWTOWN REMEMBERS OUR HEROES

Orange balloons are released at Virginia Tech's sports stadium in memory of the people killed during Cho's attack.

After the tragedy

In all the heated arguments about gun law, a just outcome for the victims is often forgotten. When the television cameras have gone, a teenager may be left paralysed, contemplating a life in a wheelchair. The death of a six-year old girl may leave a family in an ongoing state of trauma and grief, in desperate need of counselling and help. A school might be missing their brightest and most inspirational member of staff. Tragedies of this order become reference points for a lifetime.

The bigger picture

Can social justice reduce many of those pressure points that explode now and then into uncontrolled rage and tragic violence? Greater awareness of – and provision for – people with mental health problems is one part of this bigger picture. Justice can be used to heal the damage after a crime, but can it also be used to prevent a crime from happening in the first place?

THE SUICIDE FACTOR

- About 51 per cent of school killings end in the suicide of the perpetrator.
- Suicide is the third most common cause of young people's deaths in the USA.
- About 50 per cent of all youth suicides in Britain are the result of being bullied.

SOLVING THE PROBLEM

School killings are so disturbing that they make us question what it is to be human at all. If a teenager kills his classmates and then commits suicide, the question, repeated on placards around the world, is simply 'why?'. Debating and discussing the wider moral questions about the taking of human life is essential.

'The challenge with gun laws is that by definition criminals do not follow the law.'

Alex Conant, a spokesperson for Senator Marco Rubio, 2012.

Easing the pressure

The multiple strands that may contribute to a school killing may differ from one case to the next, but there are some practical steps we can all take. Making a stand against bullying can make many children's lives less miserable and may

Anti-bullying campaigns in schools and colleges highlight the need to include people and not alienate and isolate them.

This sculpture of a knotted gun stands outside the UN building in New York City. It has become a worldwide symbol for non-violence.

even save lives. Everyone can help with this issue – online, in schools and colleges, on the street and at home. Going out of one's way to make friends with people who are shy or unpopular, understanding those who are depressed, fearful or anxious, can be mutually rewarding.

Investigate and act

Many of the big issues need investigating and debating. What kind of society do we want to live in? What stand are politicians taking, and why? Find out more about mental health, medications and their side effects. Find out about the media – who owns the broadcasting companies, and are they reporting fairly and accurately? And then there is the big question – guns. Do we need more of them to stay safe? Or do we really need fewer guns, maybe none at all? Think it through. Step back and check out the evidence, not just the opinions. Public views and laws vary greatly from one country to another. See how they compare. Why does it matter so much? Just remember the victims and their families.

'We can't tolerate this anymore. These tragedies must end. And to end them, we must change.'

US President Barack Obama, Newtown, Connecticut, December 2012.

GLOSSARY

adolescent
Somebody who is growing towards adulthood. The term is usually used when talking about a teenager.

amendment
A change to a formal document, proposal, law or constitution.

amok
'Running amok' comes from an expression in the Malay language. It means a rampage of killing, often following a period of depression.

antidepressant
Any one of the medications used to treat a wide range of conditions, including anxiety, obsessive compulsive disorder (OCD) or attention-deficit hyperactivity disorder (ADHD).

antipsychotic
Psychosis is an abnormal state of mind. It occurs when someone loses touch with reality. Medications which try to manage these abnormal states of mind are called antipsychotics.

calibre
The diameter of a gun barrel or a bullet, a way of classifying a gun.

carbine
A firearm like a rifle, but with a shortened barrel.

conspiracy theory
An attempt to explain a disaster or crime by blaming individuals, organisations or governments for carrying it out or covering it up.

constitution
The principles and the legal framework on which a state or nation is established. Constitutions may be written down or unwritten.

copycat killing
An imitation of a murder or series of murders carried out by other people.

criminal responsibility, age of
The age at which someone can be held responsible for a crime and tried and punished accordingly.

ethical
Something that is based upon moral principles.

federal
In the USA, referring to the national government rather than government of the individual states.

gated community
A group of houses, apartment blocks
or other buildings that is surrounded
and protected by gates or fences for
security reasons.

gun control
A set of laws or agreements that limit
or outlaw the sale, ownership or use
of firearms.

hearsay
Evidence based on other people's
testimony or opinion rather than on
first-hand evidence.

hijack
To seize control of a car, train, ship or
plane, using armed force.

hostage crisis
Seizing or kidnapping people and holding
them with armed force, while making
political or other demands in return for
their release.

lobby
Attempting to gain political or
commercial influence over elected
representatives.

low self-esteem
A poor self-image, often the result of
depression or bullying.

media
The channels used for communicating
news or other information. They include
newspapers, books, television and radio,
as well as the Internet and social media,
such as Twitter or Facebook.

militia
A fighting force made up of citizen
volunteers or non-professional soldiers.

moral
Concerning the principles of what is right
and what is wrong.

peer group
A group of people of the same age and
social background. Peer means 'equal'.

pharmaceutical
Related to medicines and their
manufacture.

pipe bomb
A simple, improvised bomb made of a
section of pipe packed with explosives.

propane
A liquefied petroleum gas.

school shooting
Gun violence taking place within school or
college buildings, in school yards or
playgrounds, or on school buses.

semi-automatic
A firearm that automatically reloads itself
after firing, but requires the trigger to be
pulled to fire another round.

surveillance
The use of people or cameras to watch
over a building or an area.

vigil
An act of remembrance.

vigilante
A person who is not a representative of a
law enforcement agency and who takes
the law into his or her own hands.

INDEX

BEHIND THE NEWS

978-0-7502-8252-9

978-0-7502-8255-0

978-0-7502-8254-3

978-0-7502-8256-7

978-0-7502-8253-6

978-0-7502-8257-4

WAYLAND